Great Works Instructional Guid for Literature

Los cien vestidos

A guide for the Spanish version of the book by Eleanor Estes
Great Works Author: Jodene Lynn Smith, M.A.

SHELL EDUCATION

Publishing Credits

Corinne Burton, M.A.Ed., *Publisher*; Conni Medina, M.A.Ed., *Managing Editor*; Emily R. Smith, M.A.Ed., *Content Director*; Robin Erickson, *Art Director*; Lee Aucoin, *Senior Graphic Designer*; Caroline Gasca, M.S.Ed., *Editor*; Stephanie Bernard, *Associate Editor*; Sam Morales, M.A., *Associate Editor*; Don Tran, *Graphic Designer*; Sandy Qadamani, *Graphic Designer*

Image Credits

Cover design & illustration Lee Aucoin; background image iStock

Standards

© Copyright 2010. National Governors Association Center for Best Practices and Council of Chief State School Officers. All rights reserved.
© Copyright 2007–2015. Texas Education Assocation (TEA). All rights reserved.

Shell Education

A division of Teacher Created Materials
5301 Oceanus Drive
Huntington Beach, CA 92649-1030
ISBN 978-1-4258-1752-7
www.tcmpub.com/shell-education
© 2018 Shell Educational Publishing, Inc.

Table of Contents

How to Use This Literature Guide

Today's standards demand rigor and relevance in the reading of complex texts. The units in this series guide teachers in a rich and deep exploration of worthwhile works of literature for classroom study. The most rigorous instruction can also be interesting and engaging!

Many current strategies for effective literacy instruction have been incorporated into these instructional guides for literature. Throughout the units, text-dependent questions are used to determine comprehension of the book as well as student interpretation of the vocabulary words. The books chosen for the series are complex and are exemplars of carefully crafted works of literature. Close reading is used throughout the units to guide students toward revisiting the text and using textual evidence to respond to prompts orally and in writing. Students must analyze the story elements in multiple assignments for each section of the book. All of these strategies work together to rigorously guide students through their study of literature.

The next few pages describe how to use this guide for a purposeful and meaningful literature study. Each section of this guide is set up in the same way to make it easier for you to implement the instruction in your classroom.

Theme Thoughts

The great works of literature used throughout this series have important themes that have been relevant to people for many years. Many of the themes will be discussed during the various sections of this instructional guide. However, it would also benefit students to have independent time to think about the key themes of the book.

Before students begin reading, have them complete the *Pre-Reading Theme Thoughts* (page 13). This graphic organizer will allow students to think about the themes outside the context of the story. They'll have the opportunity to evaluate statements based on important themes and defend their opinions. Be sure to keep students' papers for comparison to the *Post-Reading Theme Thoughts* (page 59). This graphic organizer is similar to the pre-reading activity. However, this time, students will be answering the questions from the point of view of one of the characters in the book. They have to think about how the character would feel about each statement and defend their thoughts. To conclude the activity, have students compare what they thought about the themes before they read the book to what the characters discovered during the story.

How to Use This Literature Guide (cont.)

Vocabulary

Each teacher reference vocabulary overview page has definitions and sentences about how key vocabulary words are used in the section. These words should be introduced and discussed with students. Students will use these words in different activities throughout the book.

On some of the vocabulary student pages, students are asked to answer text-related questions about vocabulary words from the sections. The following question stems will help you create your own vocabulary questions if you'd like to extend the discussion.

- ¿De qué manera esta palabra describe la personalidad de _____ ?
- ¿De qué manera esta palabra se relaciona con el problema del cuento?
- ¿De qué manera esta palabra te ayuda a comprender el escenario?
- Dime de qué manera esta palabra se relaciona con la idea principal del cuento.
- ¿Qué imágenes te trae a la mente esta palabra?
- ¿Por qué crees que la autora usó esta palabra?

At times, you may find that more work with the words will help students understand their meanings and importance. These quick vocabulary activities are a good way to further study the words.

- Students can play vocabulary concentration. Make one set of cards that has the words on them and another set with the definitions. Then, have students lay them out on the table and play concentration. The goal of the game is to match vocabulary words with their definitions. For early readers or language learners, the two sets of cards could be the words and pictures of the words.

- Students can create word journal entries about the words. Students choose words they think are important and then describe why they think each word is important within the book. Early readers or language learners could instead draw pictures about the words in a journal.

- Students can create puppets and use them to act out the vocabulary words from the stories. Students may also enjoy telling their own character-driven stories using vocabulary words from the original stories.

How to Use This Literature Guide (cont.)

Analyzing the Literature

After you have read each section with students, hold a small-group or whole-class discussion. Provided on the teacher reference page for each section are leveled questions. The questions are written at two levels of complexity to allow you to decide which questions best meet the needs of your students. The Level 1 questions are typically less abstract than the Level 2 questions. These questions are focused on the various story elements, such as character, setting, and plot. Be sure to add further questions as your students discuss what they've read. For each question, a few key points are provided for your reference as you discuss the book with students.

Reader Response

In today's classrooms, there are often great readers who are below average writers. So much time and energy is spent in classrooms getting students to read on grade level that little time is left to focus on writing skills. To help teachers include more writing in their daily literacy instruction, each section of this guide has a literature-based reader response prompt. Each of the three genres of writing is used in the reader responses within this guide: narrative, informative/explanatory, and opinion. Before students write, you may want to allow them time to draw pictures related to the topic.

Guided Close Reading

Within each section of this guide, it is suggested that you closely reread a portion of the text with your students. Page numbers are given, but since some versions of the books may have different page numbers, the sections to be reread are described by location as well. After rereading the section, there are a few text-dependent questions to be answered by students.

Working space has been provided to help students prepare for the group discussion. They should record their thoughts and ideas on the activity page and refer to it during your discussion. Rather than just taking notes, you may want to require students to write complete responses to the questions before discussing them with you.

Encourage students to read one question at a time and then go back to the text and discover the answer. Work with students to ensure that they use the text to determine their answers rather than making unsupported inferences. Suggested answers are provided in the answer key.

How to Use This Literature Guide (cont.)

Guided Close Reading (cont.)

The generic open-ended stems below can be used to write your own text-dependent questions if you would like to give students more practice.

- ¿Qué palabras del cuento respaldan...?
- ¿Qué texto te ayuda a entender...?
- Usa el libro para explicar por qué sucedió _____.
- Basándote en los sucesos del cuento, ¿...?
- Muéstrame la parte del texto que apoya...
- Usa el texto para explicar por qué...

Making Connections

The activities in this section help students make cross-curricular connections to mathematics, science, social studies, fine arts, or other curricular areas. These activities require higher-order thinking skills from students but also allow for creative thinking.

Language Learning

A special section has been set aside to connect the literature to language conventions. Through these activities, students will have opportunities to practice the conventions of standard English grammar, usage, capitalization, and punctuation.

Story Elements

It is important to spend time discussing what the common story elements are in literature. Understanding the characters, setting, plot, and theme can increase students' comprehension and appreciation of the story. If teachers begin discussing these elements in early childhood, students will more likely internalize the concepts and look for the elements in their independent reading. Another very important reason for focusing on the story elements is that students will be better writers if they think about how the stories they read are constructed.

In the story elements activities, students are asked to create work related to the characters, setting, or plot. Consider having students complete only one of these activities. If you give students a choice on this assignment, each student can decide to complete the activity that most appeals to him or her. Different intelligences are used so that the activities are diverse and interesting to all students.

How to Use This Literature Guide (cont.)

Culminating Activity

At the end of this instructional guide is a creative culminating activity that allows students the opportunity to share what they've learned from reading the books in the series. This activity is open ended so that students can push themselves to create their own great works within your language arts classroom.

Comprehension Assessment

The questions in this section require students to think about the books they've read as well as the words that were used in the books. Some questions are tied to quotations from the books to engage students and require them to think about the text as they answer the questions.

Response to Literature

Finally, students are asked to respond to the literature by drawing pictures and writing about the characters and stories. A suggested rubric is provided for teacher reference.

Correlation to the Standards

Shell Education is committed to producing educational materials that are research and standards based. As part of this effort, we have correlated all of our products to the academic standards of all 50 states, the District of Columbia, the Department of Defense Dependents Schools, and all Canadian provinces.

Purpose and Intent of Standards

The Every Student Succeeds Act (ESSA) mandates that all states adopt challenging academic standards that help students meet the goal of college and career readiness. While many states already adopted academic standards prior to ESSA, the act continues to hold states accountable for detailed and comprehensive standards. Standards are statements that describe the criteria necessary for students to meet specific academic goals. They define the knowledge, skills, and content students should acquire at each level. State standards are used in the development of our products, so educators can be assured they meet state academic requirements.

How to Find Standards Correlations

To print a customized correlation report of this product for your state, visit our website at **www.teachercreatedmaterials.com/administrators/correlations/** and follow the online directions. If you require assistance in printing correlation reports, please contact our Customer Service Department at 1-877-777-3450.

Correlation to the Standards

Standards Correlation Chart

The lessons in this guide were written to support today's college and career readiness standards. This chart indicates which sections of this guide address which standards.

College and Career Readiness Standards	Section
Read closely to determine what the text says explicitly and to make logical inferences from it; cite specific textual evidence when writing or speaking to support conclusions drawn from the text.	Analyzing the Literature Sections 1–5; Guided Close Reading Sections 1–5; Story Elements Sections 1–5
Analyze how and why individuals, events, or ideas develop and interact over the course of a text.	Story Elements Sections 1–5; Guided Close Reading Sections 1–5
Interpret words and phrases as they are used in a text, including determining technical, connotative, and figurative meanings, and analyze how specific word choices shape meaning or tone.	Vocabulary Sections 1–5
Analyze the structure of texts, including how specific sentences, paragraphs, and larger portions of the text (e.g., a section, chapter, scene, or stanza) relate to each other and the whole.	Story Elements Sections 1–2
Read and comprehend complex literary and informational texts independently and proficiently.	Entire Unit
Write arguments to support claims in an analysis of substantive topics or texts using valid reasoning and relevant and sufficient evidence.	Reader Response Sections 2, 4
Write informative/explanatory texts to examine and convey complex ideas and information clearly and accurately through the effective selection, organization, and analysis of content.	Reader Response Sections 1, 5
Write narratives to develop real or imagined experiences or events using effective technique, well-chosen details and well-structured event sequences.	Reader Response Section 3
Produce clear and coherent writing in which the development, organization, and style are appropriate to task, purpose, and audience.	Reader Response Sections 1–5
Develop and strengthen writing as needed by planning, revising, editing, rewriting, or trying a new approach.	Story Elements Section 5

Correlation to the Standards (cont.)

Standards Correlation Chart (cont.)

College and Career Readiness Standards	Section
Conduct short as well as more sustained projects based on focused questions, demonstrating understanding of the subject under investigation.	Making Connections Sections 1, 3; Post-Reading Response to Literature
Demonstrate command of the conventions of standard English grammar and usage when writing or speaking.	Vocabulary Sections 1–5; Guided Close Reading Sections 1–5; Making Connections Section 1; Language Learning Sections 3–4; Story Elements Section 2; Post-Reading Response to Literature
Demonstrate command of the conventions of standard English capitalization, punctuation, and spelling when writing.	Reader Response Sections 1–5; Language Learning Sections 1, 5
Apply knowledge of language to understand how language functions in different contexts, to make effective choices for meaning or style, and to comprehend more fully when reading or listening.	Guided Close Reading Sections 1–5
Determine or clarify the meaning of unknown and multiple-meaning words and phrases by using context clues, analyzing meaningful word parts, and consulting general and specialized reference materials, as appropriate.	Vocabulary Sections 1–5; Language Learning Section 2
Determine or clarify the meaning of unknown and multiple-meaning words and phrases by using context clues, analyzing meaningful word parts, and consulting general and specialized reference materials, as appropriate.	Vocabulary Sections 1–5
Demonstrate understanding of figurative language, word relationships, and nuances in word meanings.	Vocabulary Sections 4–5
Acquire and use accurately a range of general academic and domain-specific words and phrases sufficient for reading, writing, speaking, and listening at the college and career readiness level; demonstrate independence in gathering vocabulary knowledge when encountering an unknown term important to comprehension or expression.	Vocabulary Sections 1–5

About the Author—Eleanor Estes

Eleanor Ruth Estes was born in West Haven, Connecticut, on May 9, 1906. She was one of four children born to Louis and Caroline Rosenfeld. Her father died when she was young, and her mother provided for the family as a dressmaker. Her mother was an excellent storyteller. In fact, Estes credited her love of reading and storytelling to her mother.

As a young adult, Estes worked at the New Haven Free Public Library. In 1931, she received a scholarship to study at the Pratt Institute Library School in Brooklyn, New York. It was there that she met and married her husband, Rice Estes. Both of them worked in New York libraries until 1941.

While living and working in New York, Estes became ill with tuberculosis and was bedridden. It was during this time that she began writing. She drew on memories from her childhood and her hometown in Connecticut. She turned these memories into several books.

Estes and her husband moved to the Los Angeles area for a time, where they had their first and only child, Helena. In 1952, the Estes family moved back to Connecticut. They lived there until Estes's death on July 15, 1988. She was 82 years old. She wrote 19 children's books, including *Ginger Pye*, which received the Newbery Medal. Three of her other books (*The Middle Moffat*, *Rufus M.*, and *The Hundred Dresses*) were Newbery Honor books.

Possible Texts for Text Comparisons

Estes has written a number of other books, including: The Moffats series, *Ginger Pye*, *The Witch Family*, and *Miranda the Great*, all of which would make for good comparisons.

Cross-Curricular Connection

This book would make an excellent introduction to immigration. Students could investigate the reasons people leave the countries they lived in, how they arrive in the new countries, and challenges they faced as immigrants. It can also be used within a character education unit on friendship, kindness, bullying, and speaking out against wrongs.

Book Summary of *The Hundred Dresses*

Every day, Peggy and Maddie wait for Wanda Petronski to play a game. Peggy teases Wanda by asking her about the hundred dresses she says she has at home. The other girls in the class don't believe it's true because Wanda wears the same faded blue dress to school each day. Maddie does not say anything but goes along with the game because she is not brave enough to stand up to Peggy.

One day, Wanda doesn't come to school. Her family has moved, and now Peggy and Maddie feel badly for how they treated Wanda. When their classroom teacher announces Wanda as the winner of a dress design contest and displays Wanda's designs of one hundred dresses, the girls decide to find Wanda to tell her about the award and to reconcile.

The girls walk to the area of town where Wanda and her family lived, but the Petronskis have already moved. The girls write Wanda a letter hoping that the post office will forward it, but they don't hear from Wanda immediately.

When their teacher finally receives a letter, Wanda is kind with her words, and she includes instructions that specific drawings be given to Peggy and Maddie. When Maddie and Peggy get home and look at the drawings closer, they realize that Wanda has drawn them. Both girls, and especially Maddie, learn a lesson about being kind from the very person they were being unkind to each day.

Possible Texts for Text Sets

- Blume, Judy. 2014. *Blubber*. New York: Atheneum Books for Young Readers.

- Cohen, Barbara. 2005. *Molly's Pilgrim*. New York: HarperCollins.

- Cooper, Scott. 2005. *Speak Up and Get Along! Learn the Mighty Might, Thought Chop, and More Tools to Make Friends, Stop Teasing, and Feel Good About Yourself*. Minneapolis: Free Spirit Publishing.

- Ludwig, Trudy. 2013. *The Invisible Boy*. New York: Knopf Books for Young Readers.

- McCloud, Carol. 2015. *Have You Filled a Bucket Today?: A Guide to Daily Happiness for Kids*. Brighton: Bucket Fillers.

- Michelle, Lonnie. 2002. *How Kids Make Friends: Secrets for Making Lots of Friends No Matter How Shy You Are*. Evenston: Freedom Publishing Company.

- O'Neill, Alexis. 2002. *The Recess Queen*. New York: Scholastic.

- Sornson, Bob. 2010. *The Juice Box Bully: Empowering Kids to Stand Up for Others*. Northville: FerrePress.

Prelectura: pensamientos sobre el tema

Instrucciones: Dibuja una carita feliz o una carita triste. La carita debe mostrar lo que piensas de cada afirmación. Luego, usa palabras para decir lo que piensas de cada afirmación.

Afirmación	¿Qué piensas? ☺ ☹	Explica tu respuesta.
Tus palabras no afectan a otras personas.		
No eres un abusivo si no dices nada.		
A veces, las personas tienen talentos ocultos.		
Nunca es tarde para hacer enmiendas.		

Vocabulary Overview

Key words and phrases from this section are provided below with definitions and sentences about how the words are used in the story. Introduce and discuss these important vocabulary words with students. If you think these words or other words in the story warrant more time devoted to them, there are suggestions in the introduction for other vocabulary activities (page 5).

Palabra	Definición	Oración sobre el texto
ausencia	que no está presente	Nadie advierte la **ausencia** de Wanda de la escuela.
habitualmente	casi siempre	**Habitualmente**, Wanda ocupa un asiento de la última fila del aula 13.
calificaciones	la puntuación obtenida	Los niños alborotados no obtienen buenas **calificaciones**.
pisadas	huellas o movimiento de los pies	Se ve el barro de las **pisadas** de los niños alborotados.
resonaban	hacían mucho ruido	Con los niños, **resonaban** las carcajadas.
contrario	lo opuesto	Wanda es tranquila; todo lo **contrario** de los niños.
apenas	casi no	**Apenas** si se le oye a Wanda cuando habla.
costra	una cubierta seca	Sus zapatos traían una **costra** de barro seco.
inevitablemente	que no se puede evitar	Algunos niños **inevitablemente** llegan con los zapatos sucios.
castaño	marrón rojizo	Peggy tiene el pelo de color **castaño**.
a coro	varias personas a la vez	La clase recita **a coro** el Discurso de Gettysburg.

Actividad del vocabulario

Instrucciones: Lee las frases a continuación. Reemplaza las frases subrayadas con palabras del vocabulario. Usa las palabras del Banco de palabras.

Banco de palabras

apenas	castaño	calificaciones	costra
pisadas	a coro	inevitablemente	habitualmente

1. <u>la mayor parte del tiempo</u> se sienta
   en una esquina   _____

2. <u>movimiento</u> de los pies   _____

3. una <u>cubierta</u> de barro seco   _____

4. pelo de color <u>marrón rojizo</u>   _____

5. buenas <u>notas</u> en la boleta   _____

6. recitaban <u>juntos</u> el Discurso de Gettysburg _____

7. <u>lo más probable</u>, trae los zapatos sucios   _____

8. <u>casi nunca</u> habló   _____

Instrucciones: Usa una de las palabras en una oración completa.

_____

_____

Teacher Plans

Analyzing the Literature

Provided below are discussion questions you can use in small groups, with the whole class, or for written assignments. Each question is written at two levels so that you can choose the right question for each group of students. For each question, a few key points are provided for your reference as you discuss the book with students.

Story Element	Level 1 Questions for Students	Level 2 Questions for Students	Key Discussion Points
Setting	Describe el escenario de este capítulo.	¿De qué manera el escenario de este capítulo se relaciona con los personajes?	The setting of the chapter is a classroom. The characters are all students in the classroom, so they are all classmates. Wanda is also a student of the class, but she is absent.
Character	¿Cómo se describe a Wanda?	¿Qué evidencia respalda la idea de que los demás niños no reparaban en Wanda cuando estaba en clase?	Wanda is described as quiet. She sits in the corner of the room. The text states that nobody thought about her in class, but they did wait for her at lunchtime to "have fun with her." It takes several days for students to notice that she has been absent.
Character	¿Quién se sienta en una esquina del aula?	Describe a los niños que se sientan en la esquina.	The rough boys sit in the corner of the room. They do not get good marks. The corner of the room is described as being noisier than the rest of the class. The boys in the corner scuffle their feet and laugh a lot. That area of the room is also described as having mud and dirt on the floor.
Plot	¿Cuándo se dan cuenta Peggy y Maddie de la ausencia de Wanda?	¿Qué acontecimiento hizo que Peggy y Maddie repararan en la ausencia de Wanda?	Peggy and Maddie wait for Wanda one morning on their way to school so they can "have fun with her." They are late getting to class because they keep waiting even though Wanda doesn't come.

Reflexión del lector

Piensa

En "Wanda", se describen a varios tipos de estudiantes. Piensa en qué tipo de estudiante eres.

Tema de escritura informativa/explicativa

Escribe una descripción de qué tipo de estudiante eres. Describe cómo te comportas, dónde te sientas y cómo actúas con tus compañeros.

_____

_____

_____

_____

_____

_____

_____

_____

Nombre _____ Fecha _____

Lectura enfocada guiada

Lee con atención la descripción de dónde se sienta Wanda. Comienza al principio del capítulo. Detente en: "se limitaba a esbozar una mueca".

Instrucciones: Piensa en estas preguntas. En los espacios, escribe ideas o haz dibujos mientras piensas. Prepárate para compartir tus respuestas.

❶ ¿Cómo se describe el comportamiento de Wanda?

❷ ¿Qué evidencia hay para explicar por qué Wanda trae los zapatos tan sucios?

❸ ¿Qué posible razón se nos da para explicar por qué Wanda se sienta en la esquina?

Relacionarse: el Discurso de Gettysburg

Instrucciones: Lee el texto. Luego, responde las preguntas.

El Presidente Abraham Lincoln pronunció un discurso que se hizo muy famoso. Pronunció el discurso después de la batalla de Gettysburg, en 1863. Estados Unidos estaba en medio de la guerra de Secesión. Se pelearon dos partes del país. En el discurso, Lincoln hace un llamado para que el país permanezca unido. ¡La primera oración del discurso es famosa aun hoy!

1. ¿Qué es el Discurso de Gettysburg?

_____

_____

_____

2. ¿Qué sucedía en Estados Unidos que hizo que Lincoln pidiera al país que permaneciera unido?

_____

_____

_____

Reto: Aprende de memoria ya sea la primera oración del Discurso de Gettysburg o la parte del discurso que se menciona en el capítulo "Wanda".

Nombre _____ Fecha _____

Aprendizaje del lenguaje: imperfecto de subjuntivo

Instrucciones: Escribe el verbo equivalente. Se ha hecho un ejemplo como ayuda.

¡Pistas del lenguaje!

Algo posible o algo incierto se puede expresar por medio del subjuntivo de dos maneras, según se prefiera: *-ra* o *-se*.

Wanda bajaba la vista como si <u>estuviera</u> a punto de llorar.

Wanda bajaba la vista como si <u>estuviese</u> a punto de llorar.

1. estuviera = _____*estuviese*_____

2. hubiera = _____

3. quisiese = _____

4. sintiese = _____

5. amontonara = _____

6. tratase = _____

Instrucciones: Escribe una oración usando uno de los verbos que aparecen arriba.

_____

_____

_____

Elementos del texto: personajes

Instrucciones: Completa el diagrama de Venn con información sobre cada personaje.

Estudiantes del aula 13

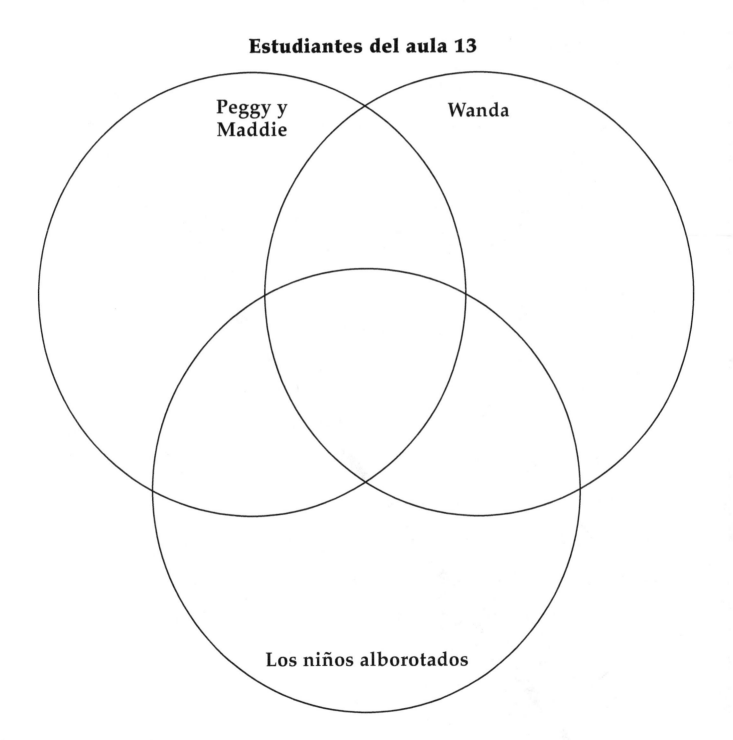

Peggy y Maddie

Wanda

Los niños alborotados

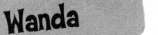
Elementos del texto: trama

Instrucciones: Piensa en quién reparaba en la ausencia de Wanda. Luego, completa la línea de tiempo para mostrar quién se da cuenta de ello y en qué orden.

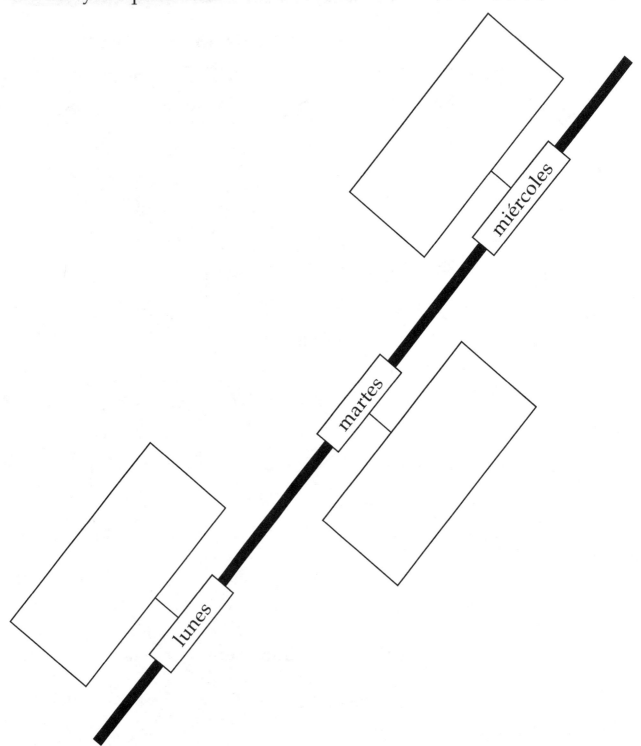

Vocabulary Overview

Key words and phrases from this section are provided below with definitions and sentences about how the words are used in the story. Introduce and discuss these important vocabulary words with students. If you think these words or other words in the story warrant more time devoted to them, there are suggestions in the introduction for other vocabulary activities (page 5).

Palabra	Definición	Oración sobre el texto
desparramados (El juego de los vestidos)	que se encuentran en muchas partes	Hay latas oxidadas **desparramadas** por el patio.
raído (El juego de los vestidos)	muy gastado	El vestido de Wanda es azul y está **raído**.
incrédulas (El juego de los vestidos)	que no creen fácilmente	Las niñas exclamaban **incrédulas** sobre la idea.
estallaban (El juego de los vestidos)	hacían algo de repente	Las niñas **estallaban** en carcajadas.
cruel (El juego de los vestidos)	malo	Peggy no cree que es **cruel**.
burlona (El juego de los vestidos)	que molesta a los demás	Peggy le habla a Wanda con una vocecita cortés pero **burlona**.
de repente (Un día azul, radiante)	rápidamente, velozmente	Maddie se acuerda **de repente** del día en que el juego comenzó.
carmesí (Un día azul, radiante)	color rojo oscuro	Los rayos del sol se reflejan en el vestido de color **carmesí**.
admiraba (Un día azul, radiante)	consideraba con agrado	Todo el mundo **admiraba** el vestido de Cecile.
aproximó (Un día azul, radiante)	acercó a	Wanda se **aproximó** al grupo de niñas.
inmutarse (Un día azul, radiante)	alterarse	Wanda las miró sin **inmutarse**.
inesperadamente (Un día azul, radiante)	de manera no esperada	Sucedió todo tan rápida e **inesperadamente**.

Nombre _____ Fecha _____

Actividad del vocabulario

Instrucciones: Repasa las palabras y las definiciones. Luego, responde las preguntas.

1. **de repente**: rápidamente, velozmente

   ¿Qué es algo que haces **de repente**?

   _____

   _____

2. **carmesí**: color rojo oscuro

   Observa el cuarto. ¿Qué es algo que ves que sea de color **carmesí**?

   _____

   _____

3. **admira**: considera con agrado

   ¿A quién **admiras**?

   _____

   _____

4. **inmutarse**: alterarse

   ¿Qué es algo que te **inmuta**?

   _____

   _____

Analyzing the Literature

Provided below are discussion questions you can use in small groups, with the whole class, or for written assignments. Each question is written at two levels so that you can choose the right question for each group of students. For each question, a few key points are provided for your reference as you discuss the book with students.

Story Element	Level 1 Questions for Students	Level 2 Questions for Students	Key Discussion Points
Character	¿Cómo se describe a Wanda en el capítulo "El juego de los vestidos"?	¿Por qué crees que Peggy y Maddie habían esperado a conversar con Wanda?	Wanda is described as having a funny last name and living in a place where people do not want to live, Boggins Heights. She does not have any friends and walks to and from school alone. She wears the same wrinkled, faded blue dress every day. Because of the way Wanda is described, it can be inferred that Peggy and Maddie likely "have fun" with Wanda because they think she is different from them and the other students in the class.
Setting	¿Cómo se describe Boggins Heights?	¿Cómo se relaciona el escenario con el personaje de Wanda?	Boggins Heights is described as a place people do not want to live. Old man Svenson, a man who lives there, is described as "no good." His house is described as messy. This relates to Wanda because it shows that she is from a less desirable part of town. Wanda is an easy target because she lives in a poor area.
Plot	¿Qué sucede después de que Wanda dice que tiene cien vestidos?	¿Qué resulta de la afirmación de Wanda de que tiene cien vestidos?	After Wanda says she has one hundred dresses, the other girls stop playing to listen to the conversation and laugh. Peggy and Maddie begin waiting for Wanda each day to ask her, in a mocking way, about the hundred dresses she has. They also provoke her to describe the shoes and hats she has, too.
Character	¿Cómo se describe al grupo de niñas?	¿De qué manera reaccionan las niñas al juego que inicia Peggy?	The girls are more interested in the dresses they have and the ones they want to get than they are Wanda's feelings. The game begins so quickly that everybody just goes along with it. Maddie, especially, wishes they would stop teasing Wanda.

Reflexión del lector

Piensa

Maddie compadece a Wanda pero tiene miedo de enfrentar a Peggy. Por eso acepta el juego de los cien vestidos.

Tema de escritura de opinión

¿Crees que Maddie tiene buenas razones para no enfrentar a Peggy respecto al juego de los vestidos? Da tu opinión. Usa detalles para respaldar tu respuesta.

_____

_____

_____

_____

_____

_____

_____

_____

_____

Nombre _____ Fecha _____

Lectura enfocada guiada

Lee con atención la parte hacia el final de "El juego de los vestidos" donde se describe la reacción de Maddie al juego. Comienza con: "A Maddie...". Continúa hasta terminar el capítulo.

Instrucciones: Piensa en estas preguntas. En los espacios, escribe ideas o haz dibujos mientras piensas. Prepárate para compartir tus respuestas.

❶ ¿Cómo se siente Maddie respecto al juego que Peggy juega a diario con Wanda?

❷ ¿Qué hace Maddie mientras Peggy le hace preguntas a Wanda?

❸ ¿Por qué no se manifiesta Maddie en contra de lo que hace Peggy?

Nombre _____ Fecha _____

Relacionarse: el tiempo en octubre

Instrucciones: El día en el que se inicia el juego de los vestidos es en octubre. Haz un dibujo del tiempo en aquel día de octubre. Luego, haz un dibujo de cómo es el tiempo en octubre en donde vives.

Octubre en el libro

Octubre en donde vivo

El juego de los vestidos
& Un día azul, radiante

Aprendizaje del lenguaje: afijos y raíces

Instrucciones: Los afijos *in–*, *im–*, *dis–* y *des–* pueden significar "no" o "lo opuesto de". En la columna de la izquierda, subraya el afijo de cada palabra. Luego, haz corresponder cada palabra con su significado.

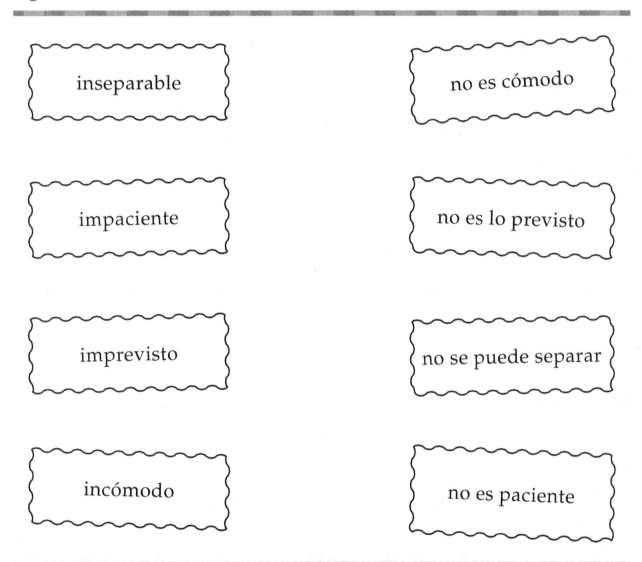

inseparable

no es cómodo

impaciente

no es lo previsto

imprevisto

no se puede separar

incómodo

no es paciente

Instrucciones: Responde la pregunta.

1. ¿Qué significa la palabra *desordenado*?

_____

_____

Nombre _____ Fecha _____

Elementos del texto: trama

Instrucciones: Completa los acontecimientos previos al juego de los vestidos. Usa el texto como ayuda.

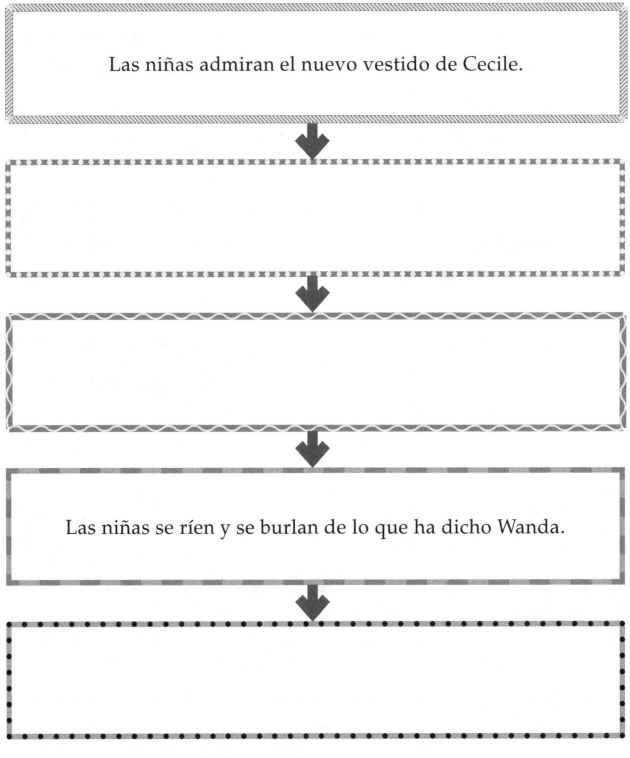

Las niñas admiran el nuevo vestido de Cecile.

Las niñas se ríen y se burlan de lo que ha dicho Wanda.

Elementos del texto: personaje

Instrucciones: Vuelve a leer esta sección del texto pensando en los personajes. Escribe una oración del texto que describa bien la personalidad del personaje.

Personaje	Oración del texto
Wanda	
Peggy	
Maddie	
las otras niñas	

Vocabulary Overview

Key words and phrases from this section are provided below with definitions and sentences about how the words are used in the story. Introduce and discuss these important vocabulary words with students. If you think these words or other words in the story warrant more time devoted to them, there are suggestions in the introduction for other vocabulary activities (page 5).

Palabra	Definición	Oración sobre el texto
adornos (El certamen de dibujo)	algo que se pone para embellecer	La mamá de Maddie cose **adornos** a los vestidos viejos de Peggy.
reconociera (El certamen de dibujo)	darse cuenta y recordar	Maddie espera que las demás niñas no **reconozcan** los vestidos que Peggy le da.
certamen (El certamen de dibujo)	concurso	Maddie se pregunta quiénes serán los ganadores del **certamen** de dibujo.
lujosos (El certamen de dibujo)	con muchos adornos y muy elegante	Wanda dibuja vestidos con diseños **lujosos**.
deslumbrantes (Los cien vestidos)	que causan admiración	Los diseños de vestidos que hace Wanda son **deslumbrantes**.
admiración (Los cien vestidos)	ver algo con agrado	La clase mira con **admiración** los dibujos de Wanda.
expuesto (Los cien vestidos)	puesto para ser visto	Los dibujos de Wanda están **expuestos** en el aula 12.
deliberadamente (Los cien vestidos)	hecho adrede	La maestra espera que nadie haya herido **deliberadamente** los sentimientos de Wanda.
cobarde (Los cien vestidos)	alguien a quien le da miedo hacer lo correcto	Maddie se considera una **cobarde** por haberse quedado callada.
desgraciado (Los cien vestidos)	que le ocurrió algo triste	Peggy hizo que Wanda se sintiese **desgraciada** al burlarse de ella.

Nombre _____ Fecha _____

Actividad del vocabulario

Instrucciones: Clasifica las palabras del vocabulario en el cuadro de categorías gramaticales.

Banco de palabras

certamen	lujosos	adornos	expuesto
desgraciado	reconociera	deslumbrantes	cobarde

Sustantivos	Verbos	Adjetivos

Instrucciones: Responde la pregunta.

1. ¿Por qué la mamá de Maddie **deliberadamente** pone **adornos** en sus vestidos?

_____

_____

_____

Analyzing the Literature

Provided below are discussion questions you can use in small groups, with the whole class, or for written assignments. Each question is written at two levels so that you can choose the right question for each group of students. For each question, a few key points are provided for your reference as you discuss the book with students.

Story Element	Level 1 Questions for Students	Level 2 Questions for Students	Key Discussion Points
Plot	¿De qué se preocupa Maddie ahora que se ha ido Wanda?	¿Por qué se preocupa Maddie de que Peggy vaya a burlarse de ella ahora que se ha ido Wanda?	Maddie is worried that Peggy will make fun of her dresses now that Wanda is gone. Maddie's dresses have been handed down to her from Peggy. Maddie's mother has added trimmings to the dresses to try to disguise them so that the other girls will not recognize them, but Maddie is worried the other girls might notice.
Setting	¿Qué está expuesto en el aula cuando entran Maddie y Peggy?	¿Por qué se quedaron paralizadas Maddie y Peggy al entrar al aula?	The teacher displays Wanda's hundred dress designs throughout the classroom. The girls are amazed when they walk in because they see Wanda's designs displayed in every part of the room. The girls all stop and gasp at how beautiful the designs are.
Character	¿Qué revela la carta del Sr. Petronski sobre la familia de Wanda?	¿Qué podemos aprender del lenguaje que usa el Sr. Petronski en su carta?	Mr. Petronski's letter indicates that they are moving to a big city so that the family will not be made fun of anymore. He states there are many funny names in the big city. The language he uses indicates that he is Polish and does not speak standard Spanish fluently.
Character	¿Cómo reacciona Maddie ante la carta del Sr. Petronski?	Explica la reacción que tuvo Maddie al escuchar la carta del Sr. Petronski.	Maddie has a difficult time concentrating on her schoolwork after the letter is read. She feels badly for the way she stood by and said nothing while Peggy teased Wanda.

Reflexión del lector

Piensa

Maddie tiene miedo de Peggy. No quiere defender a Wanda ante Peggy. Maddie tiene miedo de que vaya a ser el blanco de Peggy cuando Wanda ya no esté. Piensa en cómo se debería tratar a los amigos.

Tema de escritura narrativa

Escribe sobre un momento en el que uno de tus amigos te defendió o cuando defendiste a un amigo. ¿Cómo te hizo sentir esta experiencia?

_____

_____

_____

_____

_____

_____

_____

_____

_____

Nombre _____ Fecha _____

Lectura enfocada guiada

Lee con atención la sección donde Maddie no puede concentrarse en sus estudios. Comienza con: "Durante la primera hora de clase...". Continúa hasta terminar el capítulo.

Instrucciones: Piensa en estas preguntas. En los espacios, escribe ideas o haz dibujos mientras piensas. Prepárate para compartir tus respuestas.

❶ ¿Por qué Maddie no logra concentrarse?

❷ Basándote en el libro, ¿por qué Maddie dice que era una cobarde?

❸ ¿Cómo piensa Maddie remediar aquella situación?

Relacionarse: inmigración

Instrucciones: Sabemos por la carta del Sr. Petronski que es de Polonia. Las personas en Estados Unidos vienen de muchas partes del mundo. Haz una encuesta entre tus compañeros para ver de dónde vienen sus familias. Haz un gráfico de marcas de conteo para mostrar de dónde vienen sus familias.

América del Norte	
América del Sur	
África	
Asia	
Australia	
Europa	

Instrucciones: Responde la pregunta.

1. Examina las marcas de conteo. ¿Qué deduces de ellas?

_____

_____

Nombre _____ Fecha _____

Aprendizaje del lenguaje: adverbios

Instrucciones: Busca cinco oraciones con adverbios en el capítulo "Los cien vestidos". Escribe las oraciones en el cuadro. Subraya los adverbios. Luego, escribe los verbos a los que describan los adverbios. Se ha hecho un ejemplo como ayuda.

¡Pistas del lenguaje!

Los adverbios son palabras que describen a los verbos. Muchas veces terminan en *–mente*.

Oración con adverbio	El verbo al que describe el adverbio
"Maggie y Peggy caminaban <u>apresuradamente</u> hacia la escuela...".	caminaban

El certamen de dibujo
& Los cien vestidos

Elementos del texto: personaje

Instrucciones: Escribe un resumen breve del papel de cada personaje en el juego de los vestidos.

Wanda	
Peggy	
Maddie	

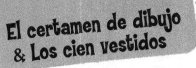

Nombre _____ Fecha _____

Elementos del texto: escenario

Instrucciones: Al principio del capítulo "Los cien vestidos" se describe cómo se ve el aula con los dibujos de los vestidos expuestos allí. Haz un dibujo del escenario basándote en cómo se describe en el texto.

© Shell Education

Vocabulary Overview

Key words and phrases from this section are provided below with definitions and sentences about how the words are used in the story. Introduce and discuss these important vocabulary words with students. If you think these words or other words in the story warrant more time devoted to them, there are suggestions in the introduction for other vocabulary activities (page 5).

Palabra	Definición	Oración sobre el texto
abandonaron	dejaron algo	**Abandonaron** el colegio y subieron la colina.
brusquedad	rapidez desagradable	Peggy habló con **brusquedad** al pensar en Wanda.
disculpas	razones que se dan para pedir perdón	Maddie desea pedirle **disculpas** a Wanda cuanto antes.
abalanzaban	se lanzaban en una dirección	En su imaginación, Maddie y Peggy se **abalanzaban** sobre alguien que se burlaba de Wanda.
disipaban	que desaparecían	Los pensamientos se le **disipaban** sin querer.
destartalada	sin orden, descompuesta	La casa del señor Svenson es vieja y **destartalada**.
resistente	que puede aguantar	La puerta no era **resistente** y ofrecía poca protección contra el viento y el frío.
inteligibles	que se pueden entender	Las palabras del viejo Svenson eran apenas **inteligibles**.
desconsoladas	muy tristes	Maddie y Peggy se sienten **desconsoladas** cuando buscan a Wanda.
determinación	una decisión final	Maddie llega a la **determinación** de que saldría en defensa de las personas.

Nombre _____ Fecha _____

Actividad del vocabulario

Instrucciones: Elige cinco palabras del vocabulario que te parezcan difíciles. Completa el cuadro para poder a aprender mejor las palabras.

Palabra	Definición	Sinónimos u otras palabras que te hacen recordar la palabra

Analyzing the Literature

Provided below are discussion questions you can use in small groups, with the whole class, or for written assignments. Each question is written at two levels so that you can choose the right question for each group of students. For each question, a few key points are provided for your reference as you discuss the book with students.

Story Element	Level 1 Questions for Students	Level 2 Questions for Students	Key Discussion Points
Character	¿Qué comentario hace Peggy sobre Wanda cuando va hacia Boggins Heights?	Peggy dice: "No creí que fuese tan inteligente como para darse cuenta de que nos estábamos divirtiendo a costa suya". ¿Qué revela el uso de la palabra *nos* sobre Peggy?	Peggy makes a comment to Maddie that she didn't call Wanda a foreigner or funny names. Peggy also says that she thought Wanda was too dumb to know that they were making fun of her. Peggy uses the word *we* to indicate that she thought she was not the only one who was making fun of Wanda.
Setting	¿Cómo describe la autora a Boggins Heights?	¿Qué evidencias provee la autora de que Boggins Heights es gris, frío y desolado?	The author states that Boggins Heights is drab, cold, and cheerless. The brook is just a trickle; there is trash, such as tin cans, old shoes, and broken umbrellas, in the brook.
Plot	¿De qué maneras busca Maddie esperanzas de que Wanda y su familia no se hayan mudado?	Maddie busca cualquier esperanza de que Wanda y su familia no se hayan mudado todavía. ¿Qué revela esto sobre Maddie?	Maddie suggests that maybe the Petronskis just went away for a little while and will be back. When she sees the cat, she hopes the cat is theirs, too, and that they will come back for it. Maddie really wants to make amends with Wanda and is saddened that she may not be able to.
Plot	¿Cómo reacciona Peggy al no poder encontrar a Wanda?	Describe la diferencia en la manera en que Maddie y Peggy reaccionan al no poder encontrar a Wanda.	Peggy is satisfied that they tried and states, "What can we do?" as if there is nothing more to be done. She suggests that asking Wanda about her dresses was giving her ideas for her drawings. Maddie is very upset that Wanda is gone and that she is not able to make amends. Maddie decides that she is no longer going to stand by while someone else is being picked on.

Nombre _____ Fecha _____

Reflexión del lector

Piensa

Al final del capítulo, Maddie decide que ya no permanecerá callada. No va a permitir que alguien se burle de otra persona. Piensa en cuán fácil o cuán difícil sería hacerlo.

Tema de escritura de opinión

Escribe sobre cuán fácil o cuán difícil es hacer lo correcto cuando otra persona no hace lo correcto. Incluye una introducción, detalles de apoyo y una conclusión.

_____

_____

_____

_____

_____

_____

_____

_____

Lectura enfocada guiada

Lee con atención la sección donde Maddie está sentada en la cama y se pone a pensar.

Instrucciones: Piensa en estas preguntas. En los espacios, escribe ideas o haz dibujos mientras piensas. Prepárate para compartir tus respuestas.

---

❶ ¿A qué determinación llega Maddie después de reflexionar?

---

❷ ¿En qué razones piensa Maddie para explicar por qué se burlan unos niños de otros en su escuela?

---

❸ ¿A qué consecuencias acepta enfrentarse Maddie si sale en defensa de otra persona?

Nombre _____ Fecha _____

Relacionarse: terreno

Instrucciones: En "Boggins Heights" se mencionan varios tipos de terreno. Completa el cuadro con información sobre cada tipo de terreno.

Terreno	Definición	Ilustración
colina		
arroyo		
bosques		

Nombre _____ Fecha _____

Aprendizaje del lenguaje: adjetivos

Instrucciones: Une cada sustantivo con los dos adjetivos que lo describen.

¡Pistas del lenguaje!

Los adjetivos son palabras que describen. Describen sustantivos.

1. la tarde — — — — — — — — — — — — — — — — — — gris y desolado

2. Boggins Heights — — — — — — — — — — lluviosa y triste

3. el gato — — — — — — — — — — — — amarillento y pequeño

4. la casa — — — — — — — — — — — — amarillento y enmarañado

5. el pelo del viejo Svenson — — — — gastada pero limpia

Instrucciones: Escribe dos adjetivos que describan a Maddie.

_____   _____

Elementos del texto: personaje y escenario

Instrucciones: Haz un dibujo del viejo Svenson y de su casa usando la descripción de este capítulo.

 51752—Instructional Guide: Los cien vestidos

Nombre _____ Fecha _____

Elementos del texto: personaje

Instrucciones: Maddie y Peggy reaccionan de manera muy distinta al no poder encontrar a Wanda. Escribe algunos detalles clave del texto para mostrar cómo reacciona cada niña.

Peggy	Maddie

Vocabulary Overview

Key words and phrases from this section are provided below with definitions and sentences about how the words are used in the story. Introduce and discuss these important vocabulary words with students. If you think these words or other words in the story warrant more time devoted to them, there are suggestions in the introduction for other vocabulary activities (page 5).

Palabra	Definición	Oración sobre el texto
dolida	sintiéndose mal	Maddie se imagina a Wanda tan **dolida** que no les quiere contestar su carta.
avergonzadas	con vergüenza	Maddie se imagina a las niñas **avergonzadas** después de que Maddie las enfrenta.
otoño	la estación entre verano e invierno	El baile de Cecile se llama "El Paso del **Otoño**".
dispuesta	que quiere hacer algo	La clase está **dispuesta** a escuchar la carta con toda atención.
comparar	ver de la misma manera	La nueva maestra de Maddie no se puede **comparar** con la señorita Mason.
enmendar	arreglar lo que pasó	Maddie lamenta no poder **enmendar** lo sucedido con Wanda.
brillantes	que reflejan mucha luz	La habitación pareció cobrar vida con aquellos colores tan **brillantes**.
de repente	muy rápido	**De repente**, se restregó los ojos y se fijó en el dibujo.
detenimiento	con mucha atención	Maddie se fija en el diseño con más **detenimiento**.
impasible	que no muestra emoción	Wanda mira **impasible** al grupo de niñas que se ríen de ella.

Actividad del vocabulario

Instrucciones: Recorta las tarjetas. Un estudiante selecciona una tarjeta y representa la palabra. Los otros estudiantes la adivinan.

avergonzado

de repente

otoño

dolido

dispuesto

impasible

Teacher Note: You may wish to write the words on a chart paper or give each student a copy of this page, so they have access to the words.

Analyzing the Literature

Provided below are discussion questions you can use in small groups, with the whole class, or for written assignments. Each question is written at two levels so that you can choose the right question for each group of students. For each question, a few key points are provided for your reference as you discuss the book with students.

Story Element	Level 1 Questions for Students	Level 2 Questions for Students	Key Discussion Points
Character	¿Cómo se siente Maddie al no poder pedirle disculpas a Wanda?	¿Qué evidencias hay de que Maddie no puede olvidar cómo la hicieron sentir a Wanda?	Maddie continues to think about Wanda, even after she and Peggy mail a letter to Wanda. Maddie even puts herself to sleep at night by making up speeches defending anyone who might tease Wanda. She also continues to feel sad.
Character	¿Qué dice el texto respecto a que Wanda no tenía mamá?	¿De qué se dan cuenta Maddie y Peggy cuando piensan en el hecho de que Wanda no tenía mamá?	The text states that the girls realized that Wanda doesn't have a mother, but they do not think about what that means for Wanda. After thinking about it, they realize that Wanda has to do her own washing and ironing. They also realize that since Wanda only has one blue dress, she probably has to do it at night after school.
Plot	¿Qué dice la carta de Wanda para la clase?	¿Qué revela el contenido de la carta de Wanda sobre su carácter?	Wanda writes to the class to tell them they can keep the hundred dresses designs. She gives specific designs to Peggy and Maddie for Christmas. She tells Miss Mason that she is better than her new teacher. She also wishes everyone a Merry Christmas. Wanda is not mean or vindictive in her letter. She is kind and giving, despite how the girls treated her.
Plot	¿Qué piensa Peggy después de ver los rostros en los dibujos de Wanda?	¿Qué evidencias hay de que Maddie no comparte los mismos pensamientos de Peggy después de ver los rostros en los dibujos?	Wanda uses Peggy's and Maddie's faces on her drawings. Peggy thinks this shows how much Wanda liked them. Maddie agrees with Peggy verbally; however, she gets teary-eyed every time she thinks of the girls teasing Wanda about the hundred dresses.

Reflexión del lector

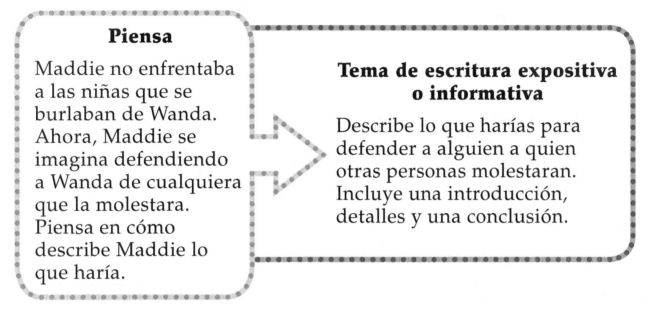

Piensa

Maddie no enfrentaba a las niñas que se burlaban de Wanda. Ahora, Maddie se imagina defendiendo a Wanda de cualquiera que la molestara. Piensa en cómo describe Maddie lo que haría.

Tema de escritura expositiva o informativa

Describe lo que harías para defender a alguien a quien otras personas molestaran. Incluye una introducción, detalles y una conclusión.

_____

_____

_____

_____

_____

_____

_____

_____

Lectura enfocada guiada

Lee con atención la sección en donde Maddie contempla el dibujo de Wanda en su dormitorio. Comienza con: "Al llegar a su casa...". Detente en: "corrió a casa de Peggy".

Instrucciones: Piensa en estas preguntas. En los espacios, escribe ideas o haz dibujos mientras piensas. Prepárate para compartir tus respuestas.

❶ ¿Por qué Maddie no se había fijado en la cara del dibujo al principio?

❷ ¿Cómo sabe Maddie que su cara está en el dibujo?

❸ ¿Qué evidencias hay de que Maddie se emociona por el regalo que Wanda les da a las niñas?

Relacionarse: época de Navidad

Instrucciones: Esta parte del texto se lleva a cabo durante la época navideña. Relee el texto para buscar información que deje en claro que es época de Navidad. Haz un dibujo de lo que leíste.

Nombre _____ Fecha _____

Aprendizaje del lenguaje: signos de puntuación

Instrucciones: Busca una oración de este capítulo para cada signo de puntuación. Escribe cada ejemplo en el cuadro.

Signo de puntuación	Oración del capítulo
punto (.)	
signos de interrogación (¿ ?)	
signos de exclamación (¡ !)	
comillas (« »)	
raya (—)	
coma (,)	
puntos suspensivos (...)	

Elementos del texto: escenario

Instrucciones: Escribe acerca de (o dibuja) cuatro escenarios distintos de este capítulo.

Nombre _____ Fecha _____

Elementos del texto: personaje

Instrucciones: Escribe una carta amistosa de Maddie a Wanda. Incluye los sentimientos verdaderos de Maddie sobre cómo trataron a Wanda. También incluye una disculpa por no haberla defendido.

_____

_____

_____

_____

_____

_____

_____

_____

_____

_____

Cordialmente,

_____

Poslectura: pensamientos sobre el tema

Instrucciones: Elige un personaje principal de *Los cien vestidos*. Imagina que eres ese personaje. Dibuja una carita feliz o una carita triste para mostrar qué piensa el personaje respecto a cada afirmación. Luego, usa palabras para explicar tu dibujo.

El personaje que elegí: _____

Afirmación	¿Qué piensa el personaje? 😊 ☹	Explica tu respuesta
Tus palabras no afectan a otras personas.		
No eres un abusivo si no dices nada.		
A veces, las personas tienen talentos ocultos.		
Nunca es tarde para hacer enmiendas.		

Teacher Plans

Culminating Activity: Friendship Festival

Directions: Host a Friendship Festival in the classroom by using some or all of the suggestions below.

Dress Decorations

Celebrate the lessons learned in *The Hundred Dresses* by using students' dress designs from the Response to Literature section (page 67). Attempt to gather one hundred dresses by having students create multiple designs. Hang the dress designs around the room on the day of the Friendship Festival.

Friendship Soup

Invite each student to bring a can of soup. Combine the soups together for a fun snack that can be shared with friends at the Friendship Festival.

Friendship Flower

Combine construction paper hands to create a class friendship flower. Display the flower at the Friendship Festival.

Friendship Bingo

Play "Friendship Bingo." Photocopy the bingo card on page 63, and give one copy to each student. Allow students time to find classmates who can sign each of the boxes. Each student may only sign each card one time, even if he or she may be able to sign more than once. Continue to play until every student has all the boxes signed. Gather the class back together, and discuss which students signed each box to learn more about students.

Kindness Notes

Make copies of the *Kindness Notes* on page 64. Provide each student with two notes. Place each student's name in a basket two times. Have each student draw two names from the basket and write a kind note to each of the students whose names were drawn. (You may wish to do this ahead of time of the Friendship Festival in order to preview each note.) Distribute each note during the Friendship Festival.

Culminating Activity: Friendship Festival (cont.)

Friendship Soup

Directions: Share a snack with friends! Follow the instructions to create a unique and tasty soup to share during the Friendship Festival.

Materials

Provide the materials or ask parents for donations.

- bowls (1 per student)
- spoons (1 per student)
- napkins
- crackers (optional)
- juice boxes (optional)
- slow cooker
- large serving spoon

Instructions

1. Pour all the soups together into the slow cooker.

2. Tell students to stir in friendship by allowing each student to stir the pot four times. The first three times, he/she should think of the name of close friends. The fourth stir should be "all the boys and girls in the classroom."

3. Allow the soup to cook on high for $1\frac{1}{2}$ – 2 hours. Stir occasionally.

4. Serve each child soup in a bowl with some crackers and a juice box, if desired.

Culminating Activity: Friendship Festival *(cont.)*

Friendship Flower

Directions: Follow these instructions to make a friendship flower to display at the Friendship Festival.

Materials:

- $\frac{1}{2}$ sheet of construction paper in various colors (one per student)
- scissors
- glue
- poster board or chart paper

Instructions

1. Provide each child with a $\frac{1}{2}$ sheet of construction paper.

2. Have each student trace his or her handprint on the construction paper and then cut it out.

3. Draw the stem of a flower on the poster board, leaving room at the top for the flower. Arrange the handprints in a circle around the top of the stem to form a large flower. Title the poster board with a friendship title such as "Friendship Flower," "We All Bloom Together," or "Flower of Friendship."

4. Display the flower in the classroom as a reminder of friendship.

Nombre _____ Fecha _____

Actividad culminante: Festival de la amistad (cont.)

Bingo de la amistad

Instrucciones: Busca a un compañero para cada casilla. Cada compañero solo debe firmar tu tarjeta una vez.

Me gusta el béisbol.	Escribo cartas a otras personas.	Me gusta cocinar.	Hablo otro idioma.
He viajado a otro país.	Soy hijo único.	Me gusta la comida china.	Tengo un apellido con más de 6 letras. >6
Me encantan los animales.	Me encanta la época navideña.	Dibujo bien.	Tengo un hermano.
Tengo un apellido con menos de 6 letras. <6	Me encanta leer.	Tengo una hermana.	Sé nadar.

Actividad culminante: Festival de la amistad (cont.)

Tarjeta de la amabilidad

Para: _____

De parte de: _____

_____

_____

_____

_____

_____

Tarjeta de la amabilidad

Para: _____

De parte de: _____

_____

_____

_____

_____

_____

Evaluación de la comprensión

Nombre _____ Fecha _____

Instrucciones: Llena la burbuja de la mejor respuesta para cada pregunta.

Sección 1: Wanda

1. ¿Qué sucede para que Peggy y Maddie por fin se den cuenta de que Wanda no llega a la escuela?

Ⓐ Ven que el asiento de Wanda está vacío.

Ⓑ Ven a Wanda camino a la escuela.

Ⓒ Esperan a Wanda, pero nunca llega.

Ⓓ Wanda no está en la escuela.

Sección 2: El juego de los vestidos & Un día azul, radiante

2. ¿Cómo describen Maddie y Peggy la manera en que se divierten con Wanda?

Ⓐ Juegan a juegos con Wanda en el patio.

Ⓑ Juegan a un juego que se llama "el juego de los vestidos".

Ⓒ Juegan con Wanda después de la escuela.

Ⓓ No juegan a juegos con Wanda.

Sección 3: El certamen de dibujo & Los cien vestidos

3. ¿De qué se da cuenta Maddie cuando dice: "'Mira, Peg... ahí está el azul del que nos habló el otro día. Es precioso, ¿verdad?'" mientras Maddie y Peggy contemplan los diseños de los vestidos expuestos en el salón?

Ⓐ Los diseños son los vestidos de los cuales hablaba Wanda.

Ⓑ Los diseños son los verdaderos vestidos que tiene Wanda en su casa.

Ⓒ Los diseños no pudieron haber sido hechos todos por una sola persona.

Ⓓ Los diseños son de los vestidos que llevan puestos ellas.

Nombre _____ Fecha _____

Evaluación de la comprensión (cont.)

Sección 4: Boggins Heights

4. Describe la lección que Maddie aprende en este capítulo.

_____

_____

_____

_____

_____

_____

_____

Sección 5: Carta dirigida al aula 13

5. ¿De qué se da cuenta Maddie con respecto a los dibujos que Wanda les dio a ella y a Peggy?

Ⓐ Wanda quiere que Maddie y Peggy tengan los cien dibujos de los vestidos.

Ⓑ Las caras de los dibujos son las de las dos niñas.

Ⓒ Wanda sabe que a Maddie y a Peggy les gustan los diseños de los vestidos de los dibujos.

Ⓓ Los vestidos de los dibujos se parecen a los vestidos que se habían puesto Maddie y Peggy.

Reflexión sobre la literatura: diseñar vestidos: ¿fácil o difícil?

Instrucciones: Diseña un vestido como lo hace Wanda. Usa como inspiración la ilustración de los vestidos expuestos en el aula del capítulo "Los cien vestidos".

Reflexión sobre la literatura:
diseñar vestidos: ¿fácil o difícil? (cont.)

Instrucciones: Usa tu dibujo de la página 67 y lo que sabes sobre el libro *Los cien vestidos* como ayuda para reponder las preguntas.

1. ¿Fue fácil o difícil para Wanda dibujar cien diseños de vestidos? ¿Qué te hace pensar de esa manera?

_____

_____

_____

_____

2. ¿Fue fácil o difícil para ti hacer un diseño de un vestido? Si te fue difícil, ¿qué es algo que se te hace más fácil hacer?

_____

_____

_____

3. ¿Por qué es bueno que diferentes personas tengan diferentes talentos?

_____

_____

_____

Pauta: Reflexión sobre la literatura

Instrucciones: Use esta pauta para evaluar las respuestas de los estudiantes.

Fantástico trabajo	Bien hecho	Sigue intentándolo
☐ Contestaste las tres preguntas de manera completa. Incluiste muchos detalles.	☐ Contestaste las tres preguntas.	☐ No contestaste las tres preguntas.
☐ Tu caligrafía es fácil de leer. No hay errores de ortografía.	☐ Podrías mejorar tu caligrafía. Hay algunos errores de ortografía.	☐ Tu caligrafía no se puede leer muy fácilmente. Hay muchos errores de ortografía.
☐ Tu dibujo es claro y está coloreado completamente.	☐ Tu dibujo es claro y una parte está coloreada.	☐ Tu dibujo no es muy claro o no está completamente coloreado.
☐ La creatividad es evidente tanto en el dibujo como en el escrito.	☐ La creatividad es evidente en el dibujo o en el escrito.	☐ No hay mucha creatividad ni en el dibujo ni en el escrito.

Comentarios del maestro: _____

_____

_____

Answer Key

Vocabulary Activity—Section 1: Wanda (page 15)

1. habitualmente
2. pisadas
3. costra
4. castaño
5. calificaciones
6. a coro
7. inevitablemente
8. apenas

Guided Close Reading—Section 1: Wanda (page 18)

1. Se describe a Wanda como una niña tranquila y que "apenas si se le oía cuando hablaba". El texto dice que nadie la había oído reírse a carcajadas.
2. Los zapatos de Wanda siempre tenían una costra de barro debido a los caminos de tierra rumbo a la escuela.
3. El texto supone que la maestra prefiere sentar a los niños con zapatos sucios en una esquina de la clase.

Making Connections—Section 1: Wanda (page 19)

1. El discurso de Gettysburg es un discurso que pronunció Abraham Lincoln al país.
2. Dos partes del país estaban en guerra durante la guerra de Secesión.

Language Learning—Section 1: Wanda (page 20)

1. estuviese
2. hubiese
3. quisiera
4. sintiera
5. amontonase
6. tratara

Story Elements—Section 1: Wanda (page 21)

Possible answers can include:

- **Peggy y Maddie**: reciben buenas calificaciones; se sientan en la primera fila.
- **Los niños alborotados**: no obtienen buenas calificaciones; se sientan en una esquina; hacen ruido; tienen los zapatos sucios.
- **Wanda**: tranquila, tiene los zapatos sucios; está ausente.

Story Elements—Section 1: Wanda (page 22)

- **lunes**: El texto dice que nadie reparaba en la ausencia de Wanda el lunes.
- **martes**: El texto dice que nadie advirtió su ausencia a excepción de la maestra y el niño que se sentaba detrás de Wanda, Bill Byron.
- **miércoles**: El texto dice que Peggy y Maddie la echaron de menos el miércoles.

Guided Close Reading—Section 2: El juego de los vestidos & Un día azul, radiante (page 27)

1. A Maddie no le gusta el juego. Quiere que Peggy deje de burlarse de Wanda. Siente pena pero tiene miedo de enfrentar a Peggy.
2. Maddie no dice nada y juega con las canicas que tiene en la mano.
3. A Maddie le preocupa que Peggy y las demás niñas se burlarán de ella porque es pobre y lleva ropa de segunda.

Making Connections—Section 2: El juego de los vestidos & Un día azul, radiante (page 28)

The book describes the October day as bright and blue, so drawings should reflect that description. Students' responses for what the weather is like will vary depending on where they live.

Language Learning—Section 2: El juego de los vestidos & Un día azul, radiante (page 29)

- inseparable: underline *in*, match to *no se puede separar*
- impaciente: underline *im*, match to *no es paciente*
- imprevisto: underline *im*, match to *no es lo previsto*
- incómodo: underline *in*, match to *no es cómodo*

1. La palabra **desordenado** significa que no es ordenado, o, que es desarreglado.

Story Elements—Section 2:
El juego de los vestidos & Un día azul, radiante (page 30)

Las niñas admiran el nuevo vestido de Cecile.
Las demás niñas del círculo comienzan a describir sus vestidos.
Wanda les dice a las niñas que tiene cien vestidos en casa.
Las niñas se ríen y se burlan de lo que ha dicho Wanda.
Peggy empieza a burlarse de Wanda y sus cien vestidos al preguntarle al respecto diariamente.

Vocabulary Activity—Section 3:
El certamen & Los cien vestidos (page 33)

Sustantivos	Verbos	Adjetivos
certamen	reconociera	desgraciado
adornos		lujosos
cobarde		deslumbrantes
		expuesto

1. La mamá de Maddie **deliberadamente** pone **adornos** en sus vestidos para que las demás niñas no se den cuenta de que son los viejos vestidos de Peggy.

Guided Close Reading—Section 3:
El certamen & Los cien vestidos (page 36)

1. Maddie siente una sensación extraña en el estómago al pensar en cómo trataban a Wanda.
2. Maddie decide que ha hecho que Wanda se sienta desgraciada al quedarse callada.
3. Maddie quiere ir a Boggins Heights a ver si Wanda se ha mudado. Quiere decirle que ganó el certamen.

Story Elements—Section 3:
El certamen & Los cien vestidos (page 39)

- **Maddie**: Maddie no dice nada sobre los vestidos de Wanda pero tampoco la defiende de Peggy.
- **Peggy**: Peggy no cree en el cuento de Wanda sobre los cien vestidos. Le pregunta cada día sobre los vestidos de manera burlona.
- **Wanda**: Wanda les dice a las niñas que tiene cien vestidos en su armario. Peggy sigue acosándola sobre los cien vestidos.

Story Elements—Section 3
El certamen & Los cien vestidos (page 40)

The classroom is described as having dress designs everywhere, on every surface including: every ledge and windowsill, tacked to the tops of the blackboards, and spread over the bird charts. They are described as "lined up." Drawings should reflect the description.

Guided Close Reading—Section 4:
Boggins Heights (page 45)

1. Maddie decide que ya no va a permanecer callada si alguien molesta a otra persona.
2. Maddie piensa que se burlan de ciertos niños porque se ven diferentes o porque tienen nombres raros.
3. Maddie comprende que podría perder su amistad con Peggy, pero está dispuesta a hacer lo correcto.

Making Connections—Section 4:
Boggins Heights (page 46)

Definitions will vary, but should be similar to the ones below. Illustrations should show the specified land features.

Terreno	Definición
colina	terreno redondeado que es más alto que el terreno de los alrededores
arroyo	un riachuelo pequeño
bosques	terrenos cubiertos por muchos árboles

Language Learning—Section 4:
Boggins Heights (page 47)

1. la tarde: lluviosa y triste
2. Boggins Heights: gris y desolado
3. el gato: amarillento y pequeño
4. la casa: gastada pero limpia
5. el pelo del viejo Svenson: amarillento y enmarañado

Story Elements—Section 4:
Boggins Heights (page 49)

Answers will vary but may include:

Peggy	Maddie
Peggy quiere buscar a Wanda, pero cuando Maddie y ella no la encuentran, no se altera. Dice que probablemente todas las preguntas que le hicieron a Wanda le dieron ideas para sus diseños.	A Maddie le preocupa mucho no poder encontrar a Wanda. Realmente quiere enmendar las cosas con Wanda. Maddie reflexiona sobre lo sucedido y decide no quedarse callada si alguien se burla de otra persona. Ella saldrá en defensa suya.

Guided Close Reading—Section 5:
Carta dirigida al aula 13 (page 54)

1. Los colores del diseño del vestido son tan llamativos que Maddie no se fija en la cara del dibujo.
2. El dibujo tiene "el cabello rubio, corto, los ojos azules y la boca ancha y recta". Cuando contempla la cara, Maddie se da cuenta de que es ella.
3. Maddie corre a casa de Peggy para ver su dibujo y para compartir la emoción con ella.

Story Elements—Section 5:
Carta dirigida al aula 13 (page 57)

Answers will vary, but settings may include Christmastime; Miss Mason's classroom; the town described as the girls walk home (grocery store, etc.); Maddie's house/room; Peggy's house/room

Comprehension Assessment (pages 65–66)

1. C. Esperan a Wanda, pero nunca llega.
2. B. Juegan a un juego que se llama "el juego de los vestidos".
3. A. Los diseños son los vestidos de los cuales hablaba Wanda.
4. Maddie aprende que debe salir en defensa de los demás aunque signifique perder a una amiga.
5. B. Las caras de los dibujos son las de las dos niñas.